nty Kingdom

The High Waters

Aztexas

The Deep

THE
TREACHEROUS
TRIANGLE

The Jamrocks

Sharkland

The Murk

Flambeaux

D1637066

Parents Guide

Hello, Arrrgh Mighty Parents!

In this Magical Adventure, Penelope and her crew will recover 4 treasures:

Venus' Broken Heart

Saturn's Ring

Orion's Belt Buckle

Magical Moon Pearl

Additionally, your young Arrrgh Mighty Reader will learn about the following topics during this adventure:

Constellations	Planets	Celestial Objects	Celestial Events
Little Dipper	Venus	The Moon	Northern Lights
Big Dipper	Saturn	The Sun	Meteor Showers
Orion		The North Star	Solar Eclipse

A MESSAGE FROM SELAH

Ahoy Matey!

Welcome to the Arrrgh Mighty Kingdom! It's an amazing place full of action, adventure, and magical treasures, treasures that I need your help protecting from the sneaky Madam Boujetto!

Madam Boujetto wants to steal all of our Kingdoms treasures to keep for herself, but if she gets them all, the water will rise and everyone will lose their homes. We can't let that happen!

You are now a Citizen of the Arrrgh Mighty Kingdom and an official member of my crew along with my best buds Raiden, Pinkie Parrakeet and Pele the Puppy Pirate. Together we must protect our Kingdom from Madam Boujetto and have lots of fun learning along the way!

Oh and don't forget to fill out your official Arrrgh Mighty Citizen Card! If you are ready to set sail and launch into our adventure together, turn the page and join me as we Search for the Magical Moon Pearl!

Anchors Up!

Your friend,
Selah (a.k.a. Penelope the Pirate Princess)

Arrrgh Mighty Citizen Card

THIS BOOK BELONGS TO:

Arrrgh Mighty

CITIZEN SINCE _____

Library of Congress Control Number: Xu002068350
ISBN: 978-1-7333576-0-9 (Hardcover)
ISBN: 978-1-7333576-1-6 (Paperback)

Published 2019 by Swagamore Edutainment, LLC

Printed in the United States of America

First Edition

PENELOPE

THE PIRATE PRINCESS

The Search for the Magical Moon Pearl

WORDS BY **SELAH NICOLE & HER DADDY**

ART BY **DUSTIN BOLTON**   MAP BY **PATRICIA HUNG**

Across the ocean and over the sea,
there lives a young Princess named Penelope.
Daughter of a King who lives life like no other
and a magnificent Queen whom she calls her mother.
The Wonder Palace is the place that she calls home,
in the Arrgh Mighty Kingdom where she and her friends roam.

As much as she enjoys the kingdom with her dad and her mother,
this young princess is far from a landlubber!
An heir to a Kingdom this young lady may be,
but she is destined to be the **Queen of the Sea.**

For this is a girl who loves adventure and is ambitious.
This is **Penelope the Pirate Princess!**

Early one morning Penelope was awakened from her sleep,
when into her window flew Pinky Parakeet.
With feathers all ruffled and a message in tow,
she told of a dastardly plan by Madam Boujetto!

Boujetto Boujetto, always up to tricky things.
Always trying to steal treasures because she's in love with the bling.
She loves and craves things that shimmer and shine,
when she catches sight of their sparkle, greed consumes her mind!

"I want them.
I love them.
They need to
be mine."

Penelope had to share the news with her friends.
Boujetto's plan to steal The Magic Moon Pearl must come to an end!
We must wait until nightfall, Penelope shouted out loud.
Then look to the sky for the plan from the stars through the clouds.

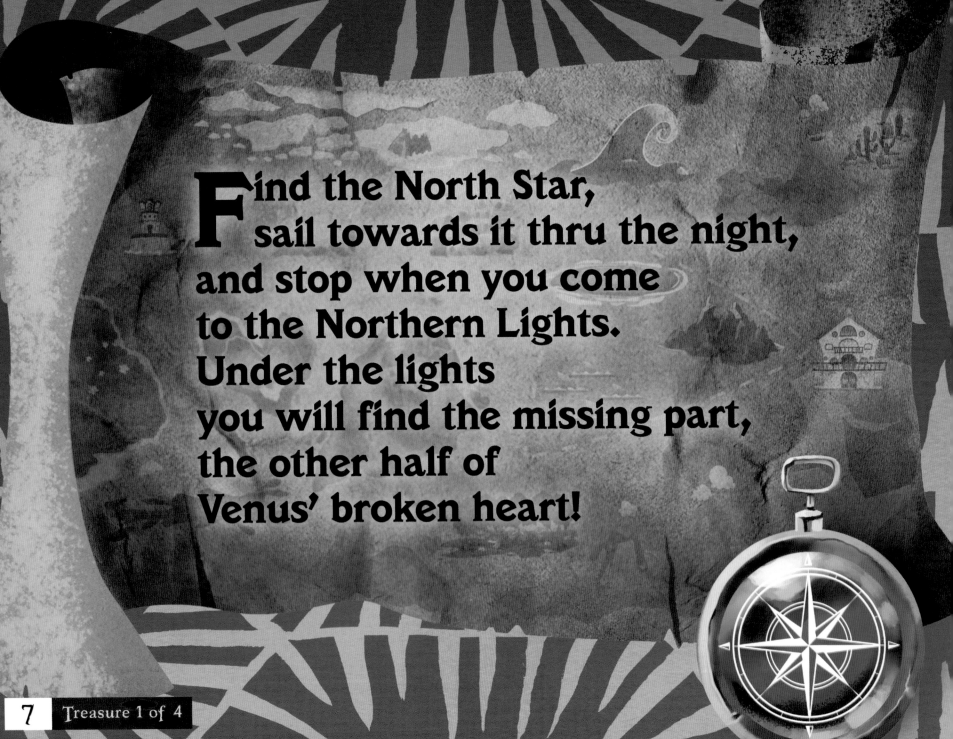

Find the North Star,
sail towards it thru the night,
and stop when you come
to the Northern Lights.
Under the lights
you will find the missing part,
the other half of
Venus' broken heart!

Penelope and her crew
now knew what to do.

They sailed to the north until the
sky danced pink, purple and blue.

When they arrived, it was silent,
quiet as a mouse.

And that's when Raiden yelled ...

"Ahoy, mateys," they heard a kind voice call,
and out of the water rose **Gnarly Narwhal!**

"I'll handle Sea Logger while you go grab the heart,
I'll keep him distracted and give you a head start."

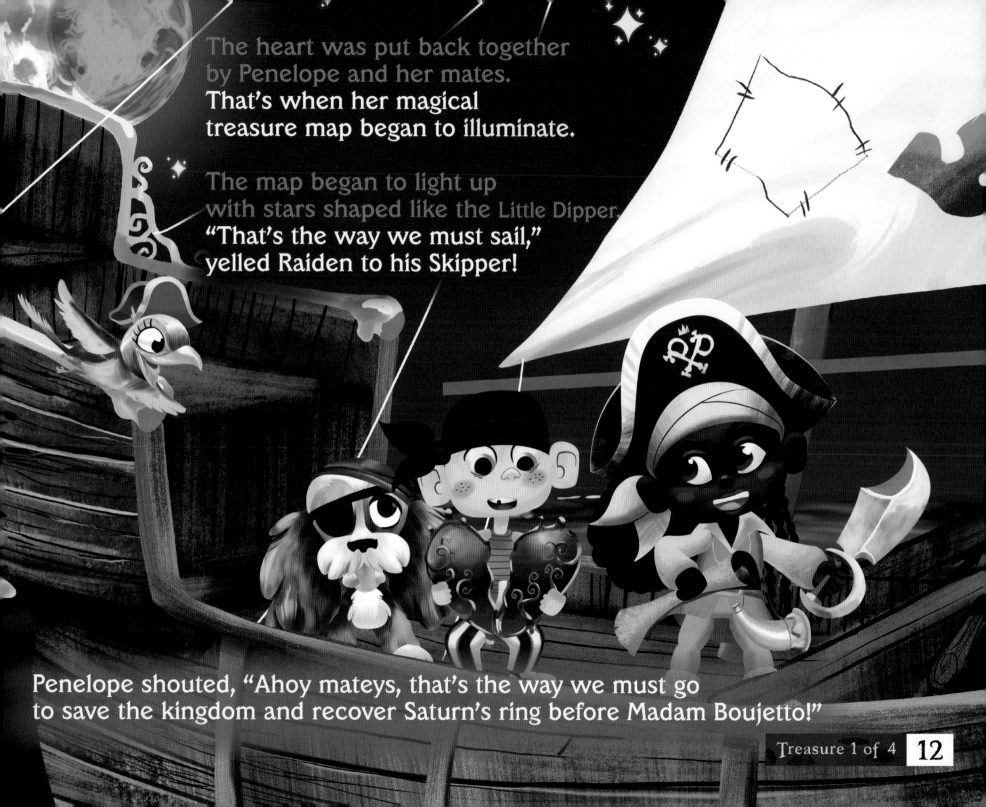

The heart was put back together by Penelope and her mates. That's when her magical treasure map began to illuminate.

The map began to light up with stars shaped like the Little Dipper. "That's the way we must sail," yelled Raiden to his Skipper!

Penelope shouted, "Ahoy mateys, that's the way we must go to save the kingdom and recover Saturn's ring before Madam Boujetto!"

Away they sailed, into the night.
They kept sailing and sailing
until there was no light.
No moon, no stars,
the sky was black like coal.
It was almost as if they had
sailed into a black hole.

What's a Black Hole?

"It's a region in space where the gravitational pull is so strong that no matter, not even light, can escape!

Where must we be? C'mon guys, let's think.
No light, no stars, this must be The Ink!
A devious dark place where no one wants to live,
a place that is run by Sanke the vampire squid!

OH NO, NOT SANKE!!!

14

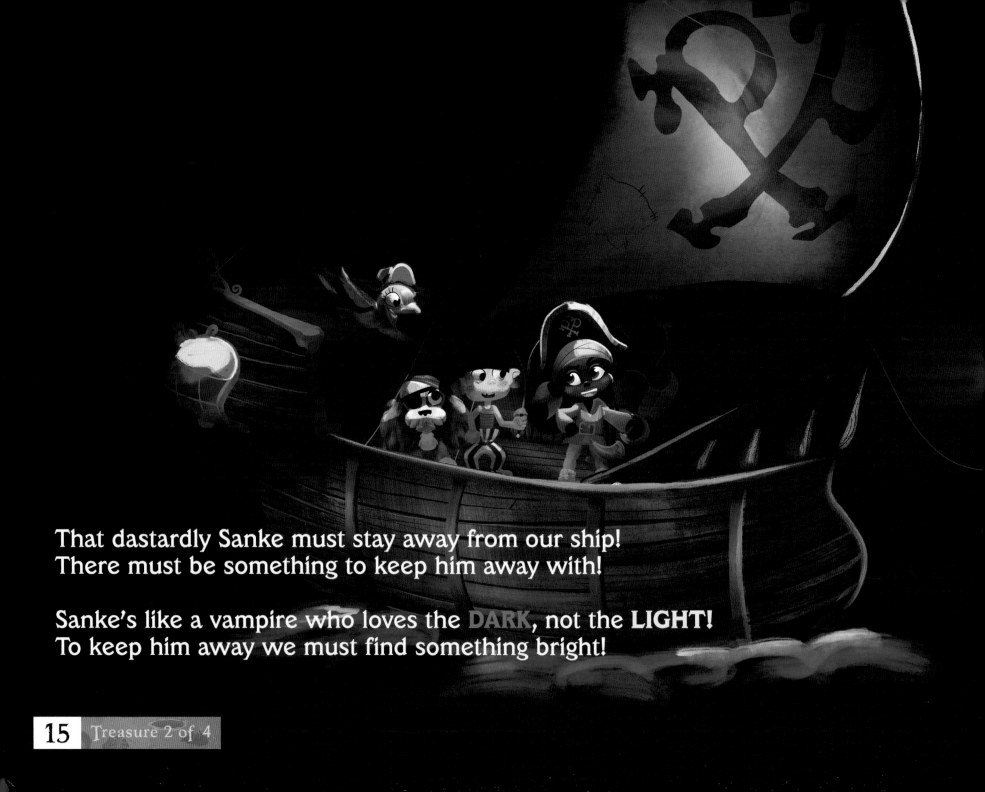

That dastardly Sanke must stay away from our ship!
There must be something to keep him away with!

Sanke's like a vampire who loves the **DARK**, not the **LIGHT**!
To keep him away we must find something bright!

Penelope and her crew searched their ship up and down,
but couldn't find anything to scare Sanke and her mateys started to frown.

All of the sudden, an idea popped into Penelope's head,
she knew just the thing ole' Sanke would dread!

She looked down at her waist as it started to glow,
and picked up her horn to call the **YUMBOES!**

The Yumboes heard Penelope's frantic cry
and spread open their wings and began to fly.

OOOOOOOEEES

The magical fairies glow in the night,
thanks to magical fairy dust that turns dark into light.

"Here come the Yumboes with their magical Fairy Dust"

The light was getting closer and Sanke became afraid.
He swam away quickly and hid in his cave.
As Sanke fled from the fairy dust shine,
a magical treasure Penelope and crew did find.

It sparkled and shone with a Beautiful Bling,
low and behold it was Saturn's lost ring.

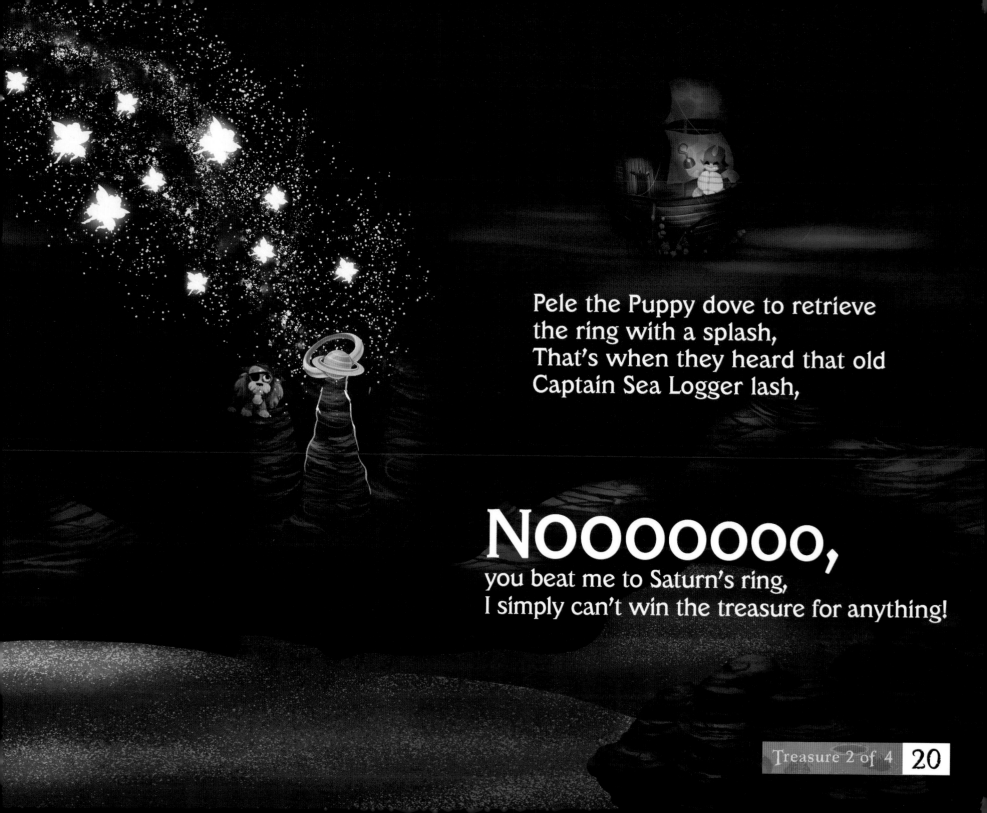

Pele the Puppy dove to retrieve
the ring with a splash,
That's when they heard that old
Captain Sea Logger lash,

NOOOOOOO,

you beat me to Saturn's ring,
I simply can't win the treasure for anything!

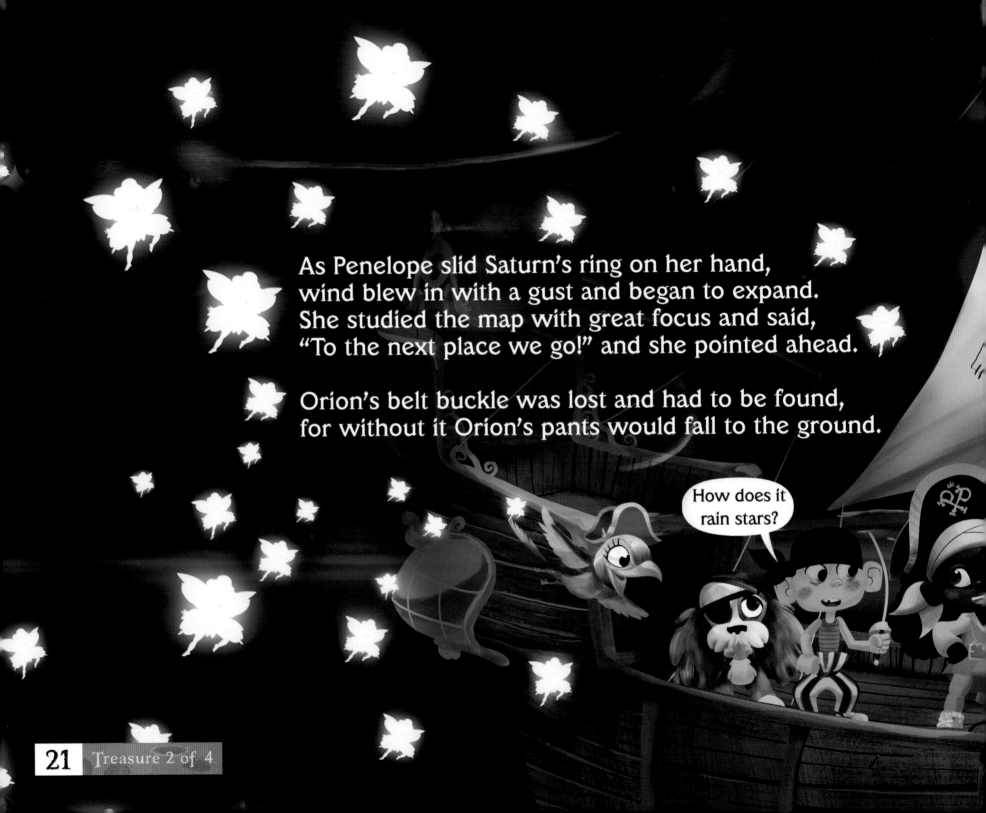

As Penelope slid Saturn's ring on her hand,
wind blew in with a gust and began to expand.
She studied the map with great focus and said,
"To the next place we go!" and she pointed ahead.

Orion's belt buckle was lost and had to be found,
for without it Orion's pants would fall to the ground.

How does it rain stars?

Look to the sky and find Orion's constellation. Set sail in that direction to find your next destination. When you get to a place where the stars begin to rain, that's where you must stop and look at your map again.

Meteor showers happen when particles in space hit Earth's atmosphere. They light up and glow and it looks like stars are raining across the sky!

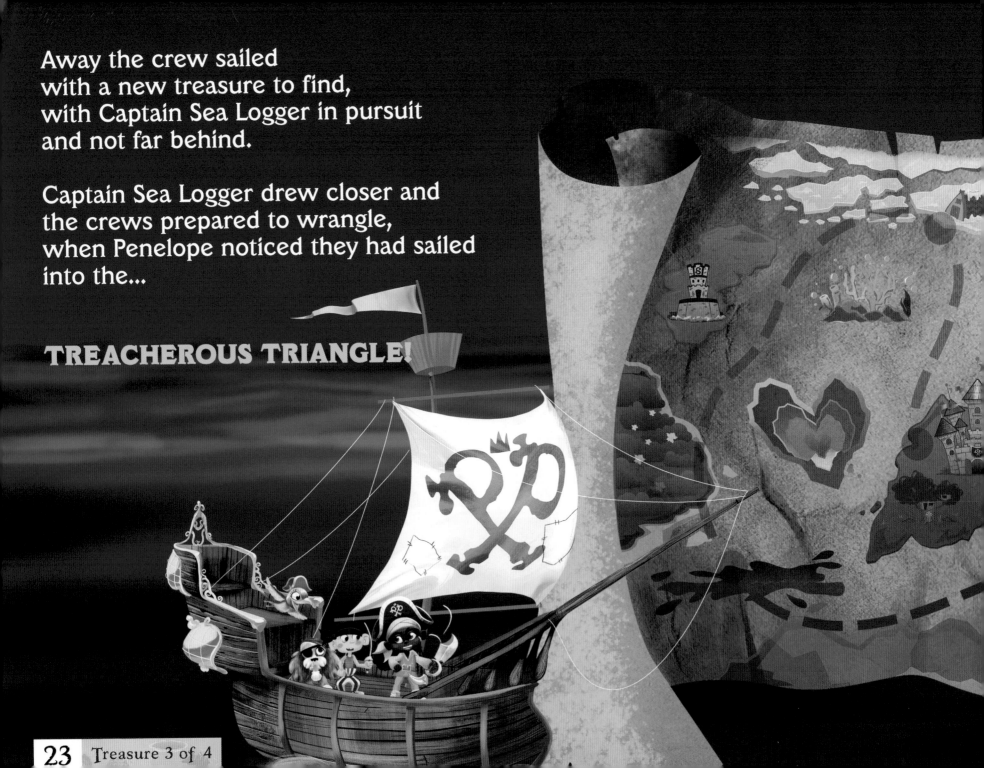

Away the crew sailed
with a new treasure to find,
with Captain Sea Logger in pursuit
and not far behind.

Captain Sea Logger drew closer and
the crews prepared to wrangle,
when Penelope noticed they had sailed
into the...

TREACHEROUS TRIANGLE!

The Jamrocks, The Deep, and Sharkland too,
when in the Treacherous Triangle
no shortage of bad guys will come for you!

Off in the distance Penelope
noticed the light from the sun.
Raiden looked to the sky and
a Meteor shower had just begun.

Penelope, Penelope, look that's our clue.
Take a look at your map,
what are we supposed to do?

Penelope then shouted,
"We are here mateys, let's stop."
They had sailed to **THE DEEP**,
just north of the Jamrocks!

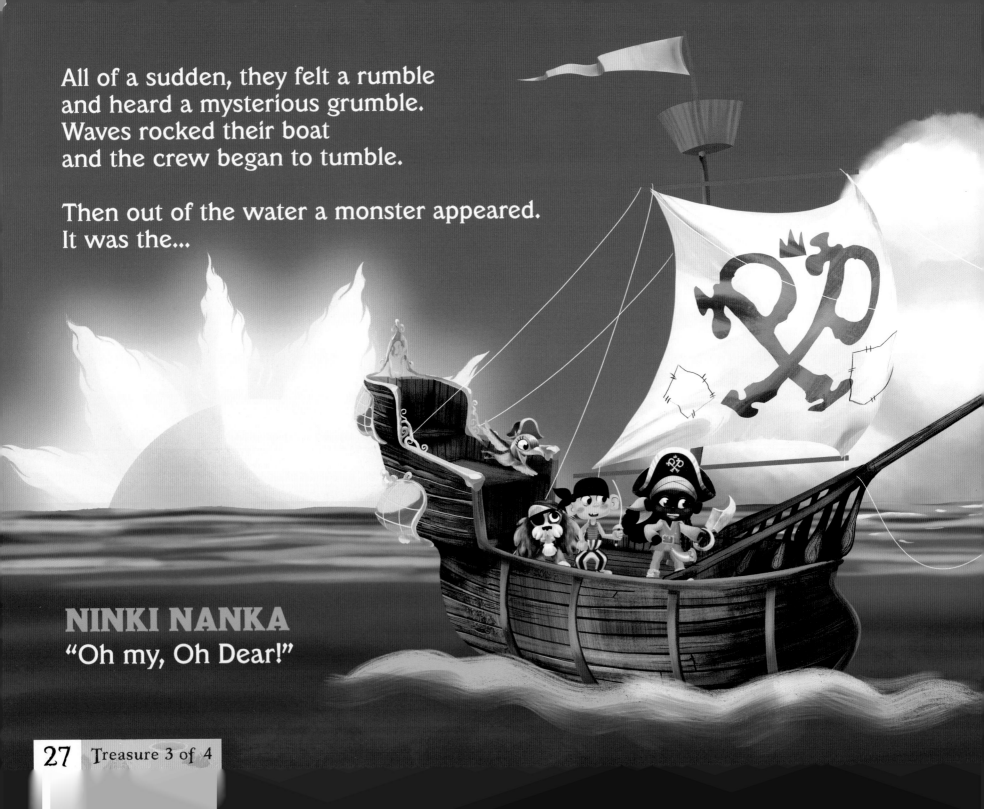

All of a sudden, they felt a rumble
and heard a mysterious grumble.
Waves rocked their boat
and the crew began to tumble.

Then out of the water a monster appeared.
It was the...

NINKI NANKA

"Oh my, Oh Dear!"

"The Ninki... The Nanka
with those big green eyes."
Then there was a shriek
and a familiar voice that screamed...

"Surprise!"

From behind the Ninki Nanka a face began to show.
It was the one the only dastardly...

MADAM BOUJETTO!

"I want that Belt Buckle… it's such a sparkly thing. It shimmers & shines and is loaded with bling. It perfectly pairs with my earrings and clutch. It's just so beautiful, I need it so much!"

Penelope and crew outnumbered they were.
Raiden yelled "Quick put your horn in the water
and summon the Mer...

PIRATES!

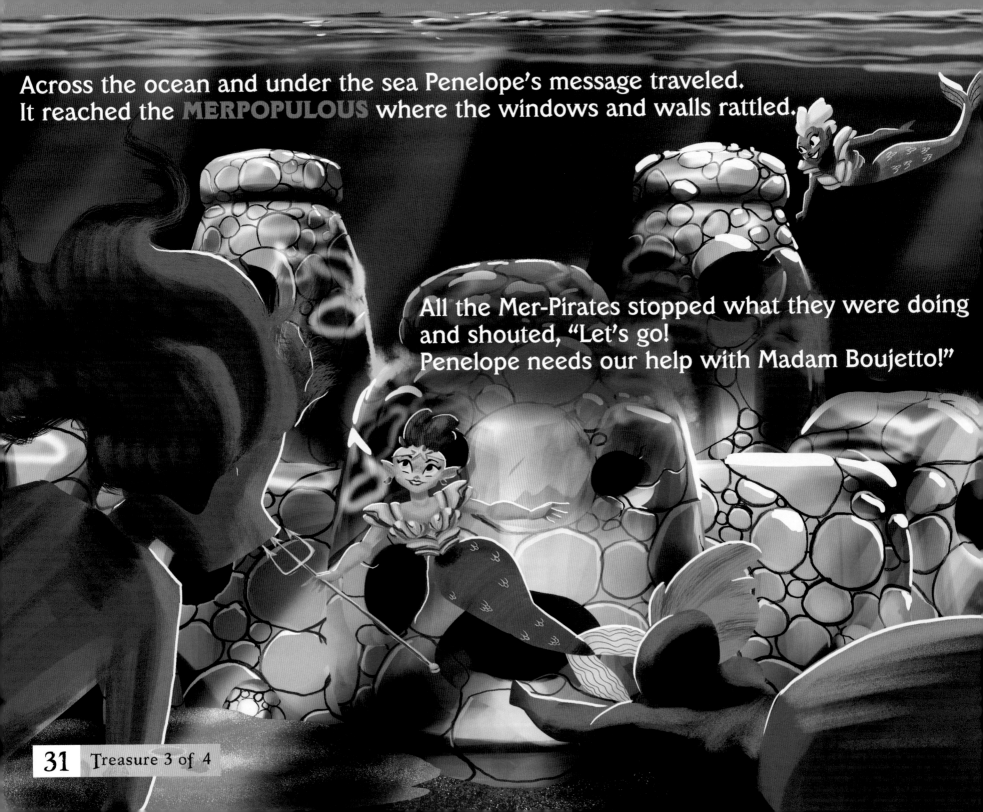

Across the ocean and under the sea Penelope's message traveled.
It reached the **MERPOPULOUS** where the windows and walls rattled.

All the Mer-Pirates stopped what they were doing
and shouted, "Let's go!
Penelope needs our help with Madam Boujetto!"

All of a sudden a tail smacked
Madam Boujetto's hand!
The Mer-Pirates got the buckle!
They'd foiled her plan!

Penelope swung from her ship and plucked the buckle from the Sea. Madam Boujetto screamed...

Nooooo, that Buckle belongs to meeee!

Sorry Boujetto you can't have this buckle or the Moon Pearl. Your selfishness and greed will destroy our Arrrgh Mighty World!

Penelope put on the buckle
and she was all set.
She looked at her glowing map,
there was 1 clue left.

Look to the Horizon and sail towards
the brightest star in the sky.
When you get to the Jamrocks
a signal will show you why.
Wait until high noon and you
will receive a message from the moon.

Penelope turned her ship to the east and they began set sail, with the Mer-Pirates to her sides flapping their tails.

P-E-N-E-L-O-P-E
Give me that treasure, bring it back to me!!!

Buojetto chased Penelope through a bay and into the Jamrock lagoon.
Penelope then looked to the sky; it was almost high noon.

C'mon hurry up, where's my message from the moon?

Then all of a sudden, the sky started to get darker.
It was not only the sky but it was also the water.
Penelope pointed across the bow of her ship:

Penelope replied,
"A solar eclipse happens when the moon slides
between the earth and the sun and blocks the light.
It's super cool and makes the day look like night!"

A sliver of light shined down onto the Jamrocks.
Raiden yelled,

"There's our signal Penelope…. X marks the spot!"

An X appeared on a rock that was shaped like a clam,
then Boujetto yelled…

That pearl will be mine,
you will not mess up my plan!

The light hit the rock
and the cave opened up.
Boujhetto's eyes glistened,
she was completely awestruck.
Sitting inside, round and
shaped like the world,
rested the beautiful, sparkly,

MAGICAL MOON PEARL!

Madam Boujetto lunged for the pearl but to no avail,
for when she got close her hand was smacked away by a Mer-Pirate tail.

Grumble Grumble, gruff gruff,
you make me so **MAD!**
That pearl would look great in a ring,
and it matches my fabulous bag.

Uggghh, Penelope,
you have won the battle but not the war.
Minions, take me back to Flambeaux,
we-will-be-back, that's for sure!

"Mateys, we did it!"
Penelope and friends cheered with a jump and a twirl!
And that is the story of how one Princess
and her friends saved the **Magical Moon Pearl!**

THE END

About the Author

Selah is a precocious 7-year-old who loves to read, do science experiments, and dream up awesome adventures to turn into amazing stories for her book series; Penelope the Pirate Princess! With the help of her parents Selah also started her own nonprofit; The Empowered Readers Literacy Project, after she noticed inequities in literacy amongst her classmates in Kindergarten. Armed with a heart of gold, a vivid imagination, and parents who embrace her vision, Selah is on a mission to help families build strong reading rituals and to get kids excited about books & reading!

To launch her vision, in January 2019 Selah organized the inaugural March to 20Hundred Thousand Books: A Children's March for Literacy! (That's 2 million books in adult terms!) Hundred's of children & their parents dressed up as their favorite characters from their favorite books and took to the streets of Atlanta with Selah to march in the name of childhood literacy!

With her first literacy march behind her, Selah is now releasing her first book; Penelope the Pirate Princess: The Search for the Magical Moon Pearl, an amazing swagtastic adventure through the world she created; The Arrrgh Mighty Kingdom. Selah's vision is to continue to help her peers get excited about reading and to inspire other children like her to tap into their own creativity & imagination and tell their own stories!

Special Thanks To:

My Mommy, Daddy, Syrai, Grandmommy, Nona, and Papa!